SPECTRUM®
READERS

LEVEL 3

FASCINATING!

Human Bodies

By Katharine Kenah

Carson-Dellosa
Publishing

An imprint of Carson-Dellosa Publishing, LLC
P.O. Box 35665
Greensboro, NC 27425-5665

carsondellosa.com

Printed in the USA. All rights reserved.
ISBN 978-1-63299-152-4

01-002131120

The human body
is a wonderful machine.
It can see and hear.
It can taste and touch.
It can run and jump.
It can think and dream.

The human body is beautiful,
surprising, and sometimes bizarre.

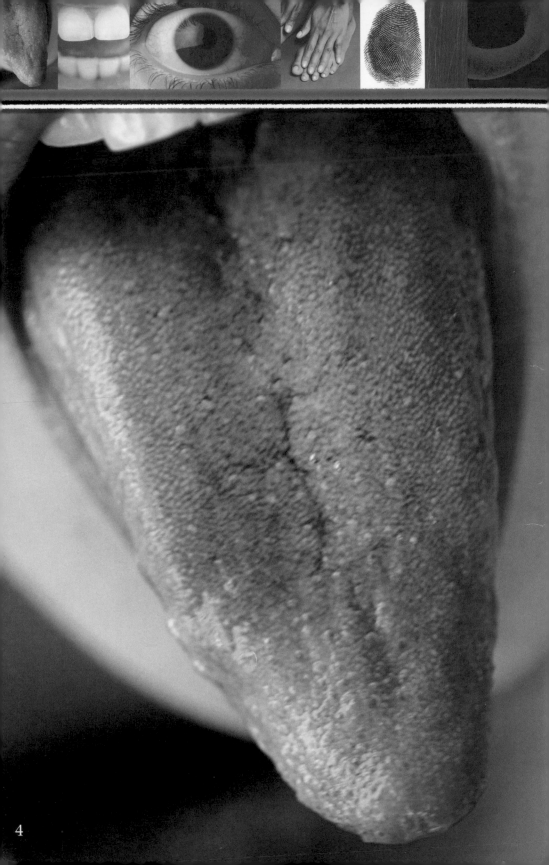

Tongue

Your tongue can change shape.
It moves around in your mouth.
This helps you eat and talk.
Tiny bumps on your tongue
are called *taste buds*.
They tell your brain when food
is sweet, sour, bitter, or salty.

Weird Facts

- The tongue is one of the strongest muscles in the human body.

- The pattern of taste buds on your tongue is one of a kind. No one else has the same tongue print!

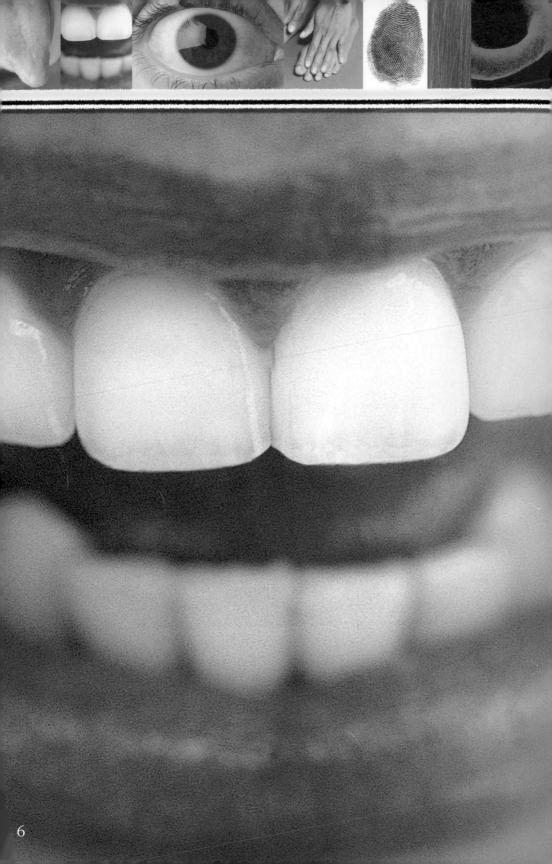

Teeth

You are born with two sets of teeth.
They are under your gums.
Twenty baby teeth grow in first.
They fall out one by one.
Later, thirty-two adult teeth grow in.
Different teeth have different jobs.
They work together to chew up food.

Weird Facts

- The hardest thing in the human body is tooth enamel.

- George Washington's false teeth were made of ivory and gold, not wood.

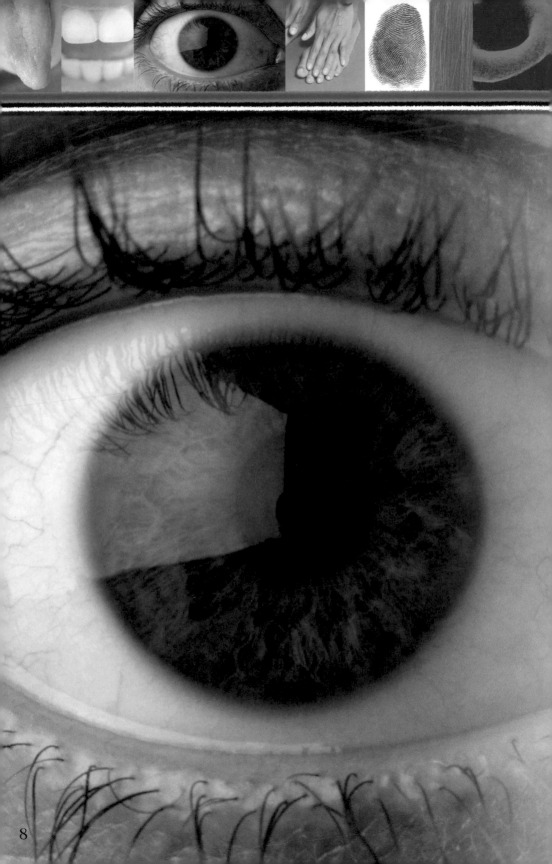

Eyes

Your eyes show you the world.
You use your eyes
for almost everything you do.
Eyeballs are only about one-inch wide.
They can see faraway things,
like stars, or things nearby, like flowers.
Your eyes cannot see anything
in total darkness.

Weird Facts

- If you lose sight in one eye, you lose only one-fifth of your vision. Your other eye will make up for some of the lost sight.

- Your eyes receive images upside down. Your brain turns them right-side-up before you "see" them.

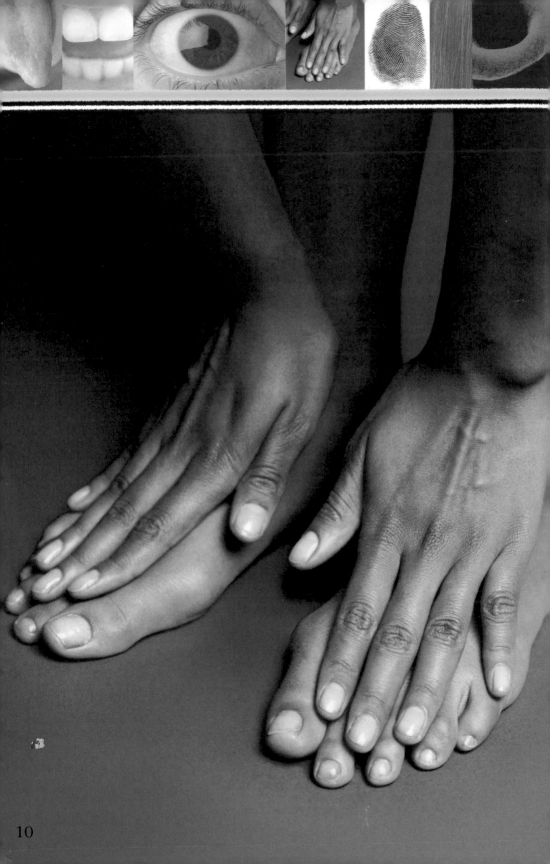

Fingernails and Toenails

Fingernails and toenails
are made from cells of hard skin.
They guard the ends of your
fingers and toes.
Nails grow from the base to the tip.
Each nail has a light half-moon shape
at its base.
Your nail starts to grow from this area.

Weird Facts

- Fingernails grow faster than toenails.
- It takes about six months for nails to grow from base to tip.

Fingerprint and Iris

Parts of your body are different
from everyone else's.
You have lines on the tips of your fingers.
These lines are called *fingerprints*.
No one else has your fingerprint.

The circle of color in your eye
is called the *iris*.
It controls light coming into the eye.
No one else has
an iris like yours.

Weird Facts

- If you hurt your fingertip, the skin will grow back with the same fingerprint!

- People with no color in their eyes are called *albinos*. Their irises are pinkish-gray.

Hair

Your hair is a lot like animals' fur.
It keeps your body warm.
Hair grows from tiny holes in your skin.
These holes are called *follicles*.
Straight hair grows out
of round follicles.
Curly hair grows out of flat follicles.
There are three million hairs
on the human body.

Weird Facts

- Beards have the fastest-growing hair. A beard could grow to be 30 feet long over a lifetime.

- People have hair on most parts of their bodies. They do not have hair on the palms of their hands, bottoms of feet, or lips.

Blood

Blood works hard to keep you healthy.
It flows through the body in tubes.
They are called *vessels*.
Blood carries food throughout your body.
It carries oxygen to your cells.
It carries away waste that the body does
not need.

Weird Facts

- All people do not have the same kind of blood.
  Blood is sorted into four types—*A*, *B*, *AB*, and *O*.
  The most common blood type in the world is *O*.

- The average person has 30 billion
  red blood cells.

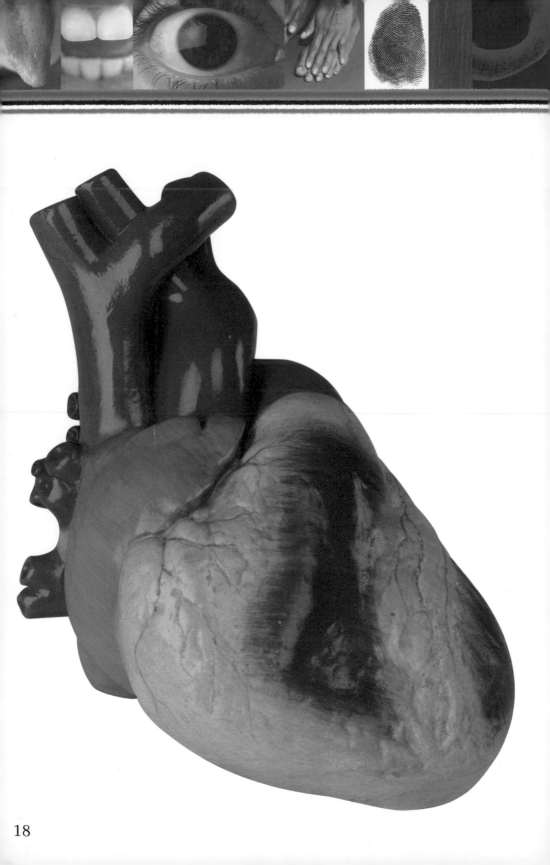

Heart

Your heart is made of special muscle.
It sends blood throughout the body.
The heart has two pumps.
One sends blood to your body.
One sends blood to your lungs.
It makes a pumping sound called a *heartbeat*.

Weird Facts

- A baby's heart beats faster than an adult's. A baby's heart beats 135 times a minute. An adult's heart beats about 70 times a minute.

- There are more heart attacks on Mondays than on any other day of the week.

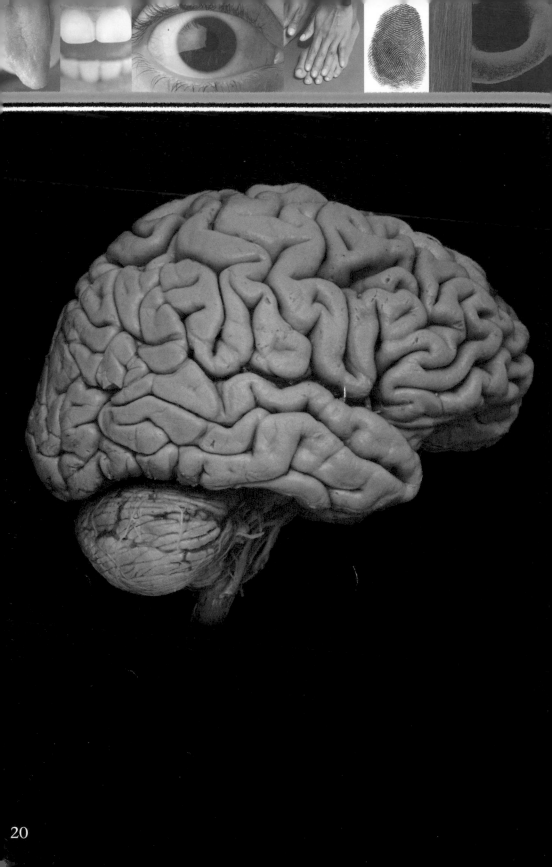

Brain

The brain is the control center
of your body.
It directs the way you think and act.
Your brain has two halves.
The right half controls
the left side of the body.
The left half controls
the right side of the body.
The brain is a grayish-pink color.
It weighs about three pounds.

Weird Facts

- The brain is made of nerve cells. Yet, it has no sensory nerves of its own. Your brain cannot feel pleasure or pain.

- The brain is wrinkled. This allows it to fit inside the skull.

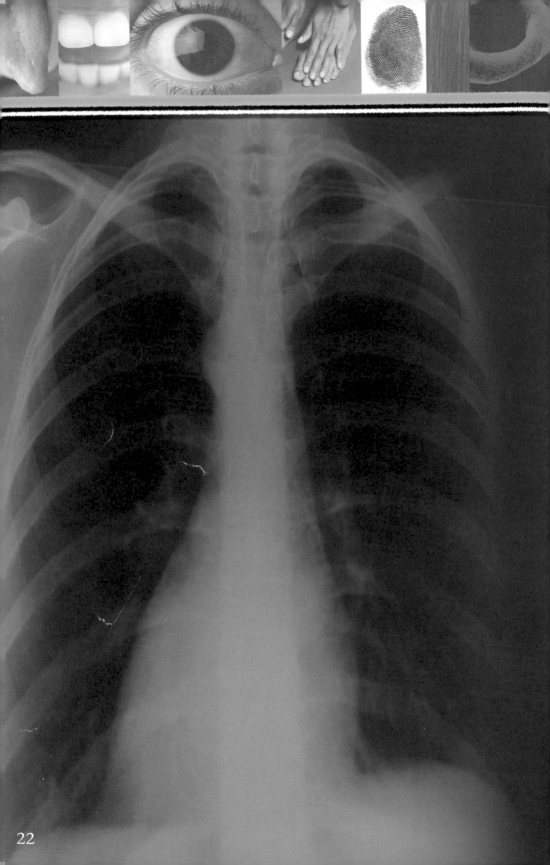

Lungs

Your lungs help you breathe.
They keep you alive.
The body cannot hold onto air
for a long time.
It always needs a new supply.
When you breathe in,
your lungs get bigger.
Air flows into your body.
Fresh air gives you power
to work and play.

Weird Facts

- No matter how hard you breathe out, you cannot force all the air out of your lungs.

- There are seven million alveoli, or tiny air sacs, in your lungs. If spread out flat, they could cover a tennis court.

23

24

Muscles

Your body has over 600 muscles.
These muscles work together.
They stretch and bend to help you move.
When muscles are used, they grow bigger.
Muscles also need rest, just like you.

Weird Facts

- You use muscles in your sleep. People change position about 35 times a night.

- Without muscles, your face would have no expression.

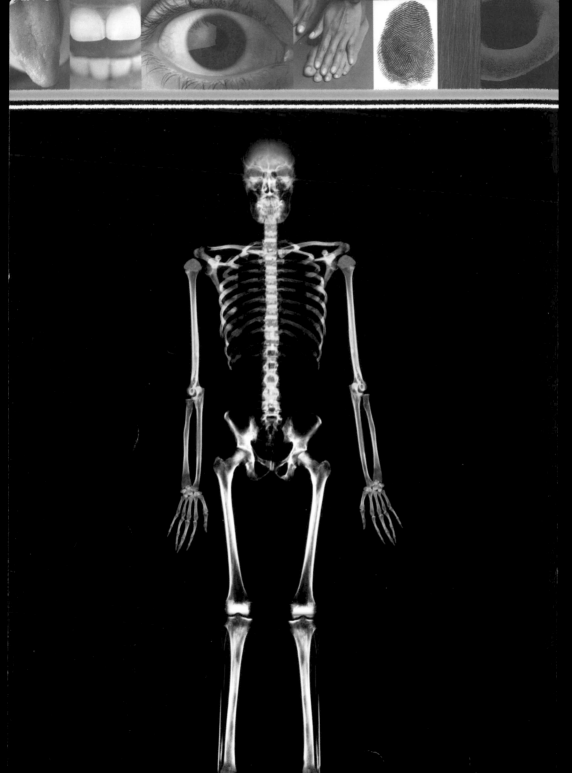

Skeleton

Walls give a house its shape.
The skeleton gives your body its shape.
There are 206 bones in the skeleton.
They guard your heart, brain, and lungs.
When two bones come together,
they form a joint.
Joints let you bend, walk, and run.

Weird Facts

- Almost 25 percent of your bones are in your feet!

- Babies are born with 300 bones. Adults have 206 bones. As you grow, some bones join together.

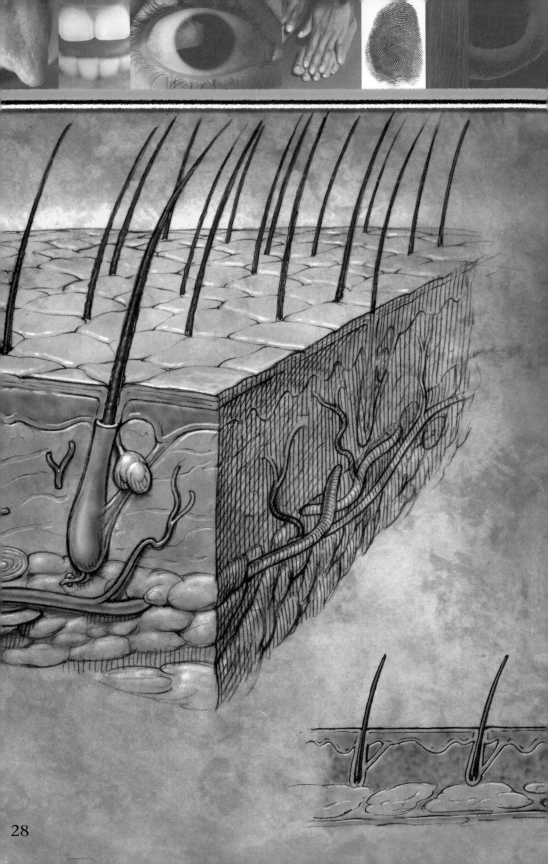

Skin

Your skin is the largest organ
in your body.
It helps you stay healthy.
Your skin keeps out dirt and germs.
It keeps in body fluids.
It also keeps your body from getting
too warm or too cold.
New skin grows all the time.

- Every hour, a person loses about 600,000 skin cells.

- There are 45 miles of nerves in your skin.